TEEN ACTIVISTS

YOUTH CHANGING THE WORLD

Barbara Sheen

San Diego, CA

About the Author

Barbara Sheen is the author of 110 books for young people. She lives in New Mexico with her family. In her spare time she likes to swim, garden, walk, cook, and read.

© 2023 ReferencePoint Press, Inc.
Printed in the United States

For more information, contact:
ReferencePoint Press, Inc.
PO Box 27779
San Diego, CA 92198
www.ReferencePointPress.com

ALL RIGHTS RESERVED.
No part of this work covered by the copyright hereon may be reproduced or used in any form or by any means—graphic, electronic, or mechanical, including photocopying, recording, taping, web distribution, or information storage retrieval systems—without the written permission of the publisher.

LIBRARY OF CONGRESS CATALOGING-IN-PUBLICATION DATA

Names: Sheen, Barbara, author.
Title: Teen activists : youth changing the world / Barbara Sheen.
Description: San Diego, CA : ReferencePoint Press, [2023] | Includes
  bibliographical references and index.
Identifiers: LCCN 2022002467 (print) | LCCN 2022002468 (ebook) | ISBN
  9781678203566 (library binding) | ISBN 9781678203573 (ebook)
Subjects: LCSH: Youth--Political activity--Juvenile literature. | Social
  action--Juvenile literature. | Political participation--Juvenile
  literature.
Classification: LCC HQ799.2.P6 S495 2023 (print) | LCC HQ799.2.P6 (ebook)
  | DDC 305.235--dc23/eng/20220311
LC record available at https://lccn.loc.gov/2022002467
LC ebook record available at https://lccn.loc.gov/2022002468

CONTENTS

Introduction   4
Powerful Voices

Chapter One   8
Protecting the Earth

Chapter Two   20
Ending Gun Violence

Chapter Three   31
Battling for Racial Justice

Chapter Four   43
Improving Children's Lives

Source Notes	55
Organizations and Websites	58
For Further Research	60
Index	61
Picture Credits	64

INTRODUCTION

Powerful Voices

Autumn Peltier (born 2004) is a member of Canada's First Nations. When she was eight years old, she attended a gathering of indigenous people at the Serpent River First Nation in Ontario. When she saw signs warning attendees that it was unsafe to drink the tap water, she was surprised to learn that not all First Nation communities have access to clean water. Right then, she decided to stand up for water issues.

She turned to her great-aunt, Josephine Mandamin, a water protection activist, for guidance. Under her aunt's mentorship, Peltier began giving speeches at community events and soon became well known among Canada's native people. In 2016 she was chosen by the Assembly of First Nations to present Prime Minster Justin Trudeau with a ceremonial water bowl to symbolize his responsibility to protect Canada's waterways. Instead of silently handing him the bowl as planned, she scolded the leader for his support of oil pipelines and mining projects, which often contaminate groundwater.

Peltier's outspokenness brought her global recognition. She has since addressed the United Nations General Assembly, been the subject of a documentary film, and been named chief water commissioner for the forty-tribe Anishinabek Nation. Thus far, her work has helped more than eighty First Nation communities gain access to clean water. But she is not yet finished. She is working to protect the world's water supplies so that every human has access to clean water.

Warriors for Change

Among Canada's First Nations, Peltier is known as a "water warrior." Activists are, indeed, warriors for change. They take strong actions to support social and political causes that they feel passionate about. This passion, according to teen activist Chanice McClover-Lee, "is not always something that you love. It could be something that makes you angry to the point where you feel you absolutely have to do something about it. . . . [Or, it] can happen as a result of a tragedy."[1]

Anyone can be an activist, no matter their race, gender, or age. As a matter of fact, historically, teen activists have played an important role in changing the world. For instance, in 1963 more than one thousand students walked out of schools all over Birmingham, Alabama, in a nonviolent demonstration against racial segregation. The event is known as the Children's March or Children's Crusade. On the first day of the march, hundreds of young people were arrested. Undaunted, more youths joined the protest the next day. The police used dogs, high-pressure fire hoses, and clubs to disperse them. The young protesters' resolve and courage moved President John F. Kennedy to support passage of the Civil Rights Act. Similarly, in the 1960s and 1970s, teen activists were instrumental in ending the Vietnam War and the military draft. During the 2010s young people in the Arab world organized antigovernment protests that resulted in the downfall of corrupt dictators in Egypt, Libya, Tunisia, and Yemen.

Modern teen activists are following in their predecessors' footsteps. They support a wide range of causes. In many cases something that threatened their own safety or their future sparked their activism. For example, Native American gun control activist

Jazmine Wildcat was deeply troubled when her grandfather, who suffers from post-traumatic stress disorder, threatened to shoot himself. The incident led her to advocate for stricter background checks of prospective gun owners, so that mentally unstable individuals do not have access to firearms.

Working Hard

Activists admit that changing the world is not easy. Successful activism makes use of many skills. Activists need to know how to research issues; good planning enables them to organize and publicize protest events, and learning public speaking techniques helps when they give speeches. They lobby politicians and circulate petitions. Some write articles and books, host podcasts, make documentary films, or create art and music to promote their cause. Most young activists begin their work at the local level, tackling issues in their own schools like bullying, discrimination,

Autumn Peltier (pictured speaking in Monaco) has been an activist since she was just eight years old. She has helped more than eighty indigenous communities gain access to clean water.

and noninclusive curricula. Some expand their work to the national and international level and to additional causes that intersect with their original mission. For example, Peltier also takes on mental health, climate change, and racial justice issues, all of which impact First Nations communities.

> "Most of my life (and the lives of all the youth activists I know and work with) consists of trying to get through my inbox while juggling homework and extracurriculars."[3]
>
> —Jamie Margolin, climate change activist

Through their work young activists acquire organizational skills and develop confidence. But their work is not without peril. They are often ridiculed, harassed, and threatened by individuals who oppose their work. In some countries individuals face imprisonment simply for protesting. Plus, because of their youth, teen activists are frequently underestimated, patronized, and/or objectified. Climate change activist Jamie Margolin recalls "a fossil fuel lobbyist creepily grabbing my shoulder and calling me sweetie."[2]

Student activists must also keep up with their schoolwork while balancing commitments they have made to their causes. "Most of my life (and the lives of all the youth activists I know and work with) consists of trying to get through my inbox while juggling homework and extracurriculars,"[3] Margolin explains.

Yet despite the challenges they face, teen activists persist. They are working to secure a better future for themselves and for those who come after them. That, they say, is worth the effort.

CHAPTER ONE

Protecting the Earth

On August 9, 2021, the United Nations' Intergovernmental Panel on Climate Change released a report in which it issued a "code red for humanity."[4] The report warned that unless urgent action is taken, human-caused climate change is set to bring about unprecedented problems for the planet. Although dire, the report did not come as a surprise to young people throughout the world, who face an uncertain future due to the threat. A 2021 British survey asked ten thousand young people ages sixteen to twenty-five, in a total of ten countries, how they felt about climate change. Sixty percent of respondents said they were very or extremely worried about the problem, and 65 percent said that their nation's government was failing to adequately address their concerns. Because they are concerned about the future, many young activists have made it their mission to slow or stop climate change. They are demanding that world leaders take action to protect their future. As Canada's Autumn Peltier explains, "Kids all over the world have to pay for mistakes we didn't even make. This is our future."[5]

A Dangerous Problem

Climate change is one of many environmental issues young activists are tackling. Most of these issues are interconnected. *Cli-*

mate change refers to a long-term change in global or regional climate patterns. The term is commonly used to describe the warming of the earth's atmosphere, which is mainly attributed to human activity such as deforestation and the burning of fossil fuels. Both practices increase the level of heat-trapping carbon dioxide in the atmosphere.

The effects of climate change are already being felt throughout the world. Heat waves, droughts, wildfires, floods, storms, and other extreme weather events have become more frequent, prolonged, and severe. Plus, because the oceans are warming, ice sheets and glaciers are shrinking, and sea levels have risen to record levels. Left unchecked, climate change will impact the length of growing seasons and agricultural productivity. People's livelihoods, human and animal migration, public health, and the global economy will be affected. Moreover, whole parts of the world could become uninhabitable, ecosystems could collapse, and many animals could face extinction.

Although it would seem that such a threat would cause people everywhere to demand action, this is not the case. The fossil fuel industry has argued that the threat is greatly exaggerated and that proposed regulations will destroy jobs and hurt the economy. As a result, climate change has become a hot political issue, with lawmakers who support regulations battling those who dismiss the threat. Activists such as Greta Thunberg (born in 2003) are frustrated by lawmakers who seem to be ignoring the reality of climate change. In her book, *No One Is Too Small to Make a Difference*, Thunberg wrote, "Some say we [climate activists] should . . . leave everything to our politicians and just vote for change. . . . But what do we do when there is no political will? What do we do when the politics needed are nowhere in sight?"[6]

> "Some say we [climate activists] should . . . leave everything to our politicians and just vote for change. . . . But what do we do when there is no political will? What do we do when the politics needed are nowhere in sight?"[6]
>
> —Greta Thunberg, climate activist

Leading the Movement

Facing an ominous future, hundreds of thousands of young people all over the world have taken a variety of actions to counter climate change. Many of them were inspired by Thunberg, a Swedish girl whose courage and dedication spearheaded a global youth climate movement. Thunberg first learned about climate change when she was just eight years old. She could not understand why more was not being done about it. Over the next three years, thoughts about the issue plagued her. After viewing a documentary on the topic, she became so depressed that she stopped speaking and eating. She was diagnosed with Asperger's syndrome, a form of autism that frequently causes individuals to fixate on a single topic to the exclusion of other interests.

For Thunberg, that single topic is climate change. Although some young people might think that having a mental health challenge like autism would interfere with being an activist, Thunberg

Many teen activists take on issues related to climate change, which is already causing many problems around the world. Emissions from cars, trucks, and buses like these in San Francisco, are a major cause of climate change.

Making Activism Personal

Organizing, marching, and speaking out are only part of the ways young climate change activists are tackling the climate crisis. For most, saving the environment is a part of their daily lives. Thunberg, for example, became a vegan—meaning she eats only plant-based foods. Vegans say that they help the environment because raising plants to eat uses less water and energy than raising livestock does. Raising livestock contributes to air pollution as well. Vegans also say that forests, which are cut down to make room for ranches, can be saved if people consume less meat. Thunberg also refuses to travel by air because airplanes are responsible for high emissions of greenhouse gases. In 2019, when she traveled from Sweden to the United States to address the United Nations, rather than flying, she spent two weeks crossing the ocean on a sailboat that was equipped with solar panels to generate whatever electrical power was needed. Thunberg also refrains from buying new clothes, which she feels is wasteful. Instead, she wears used clothing made of sustainable, recycled material.

says that it is her superpower. Her focus on climate change has made her a climate expert. In a 2021 interview, she explained, "A lot of people with autism have a special interest that they can sit and do for an eternity without getting bored. It's a very useful thing sometimes. Autism can be something that holds you back, but . . . if . . . you feel you have a purpose, then it can be something you can use for good. And I think that I'm doing that now."[7]

Armed with a massive amount of knowledge about climate change, she decided to skip school to protest Sweden's climate policies. She encouraged her classmates to join her, but they were uninterested. This did not alter her commitment to change. Carrying a homemade sign that read "School Strike for Climate," on August 20, 2018, she began a one-person protest outside the Swedish parliament. Even though her parents and many of her teachers did not approve of her missing school, she continued demonstrating every day for the next three weeks. ""What am I going to learn in school?" she said in response to those who disapproved of her strike. "Facts don't matter any more, politicians aren't listening to the scientists, so why should I learn?"[8]

Thunberg posted a selfie on social media on the first day of her solo strike, and a local newspaper ran an article about her. In a matter of days, her campaign went viral, making her an international sensation. After three weeks of daily protests, she returned to class but vowed to continue her school strike every Friday. She called her campaign Fridays for Future (FFF), and she urged students all over the world to follow her lead. Not long after this, she was asked to speak at a climate rally in Stockholm, Sweden. Although she did not like being the center of attention, her direct and impassioned words moved other young people to take up the cause. By 2019, FFF had become a global movement. Building on the movement, in September 2019 Thunberg coordinated a series of international school strikes, which became known as the Global Week for Future. An estimated 6 million people took part in the protests, making the event the largest climate strike in world history. Thunberg also continued to speak at climate rallies and major world events such as the 2021 Youth Climate Summit in Italy.

Indeed, since starting her campaign, Thunberg has addressed the United Nations, the World Economic Forum, the US Congress, and leaders of the European Union, and other government and world bodies. She received dozens of accolades, including being nominated for the Nobel Peace Prize for three consecutive years. She has also been dismissed and insulted by individuals, journalists, and world leaders who do not share her views. But they have not intimidated or silenced her. The determined young woman refuses to quit until every nation takes real action to end climate change. "We need to get angry and understand what is at stake," she says. "And then we need to transform that anger into action and to stand together united and just never give up."[9]

Fighting for Climate Justice

Throughout her campaign, Thunberg has battled for climate justice. Advocates for climate justice demand that wealthy nations

In 2018, Swedish activist Greta Thunberg (pictured center at a demonstration in Stockholm) started skipping school every Friday to protest her government's climate policies. Young people around the world quickly followed her example, and the Fridays For Future movement began.

and industries that contribute the most to carbon dioxide emissions provide assistance to vulnerable communities that contribute little to the problem but are disproportionately impacted by it and are the least able to deal with the consequences, such as floods, droughts, and other natural disasters related to climate change. Moreover, without home cooling systems or running water, they are more likely to suffer from heat-related illnesses caused by prolonged heat waves.

Yusuf Baluch (born 2004) is leading the battle to help such vulnerable people and communities. Baluch lives in a small, economically challenged village in Balochistan, Pakistan. His and other villages in the region have been suffering from the impact of climate change for years. Floods have repeatedly destroyed local communities; in other years, heat waves and prolonged droughts have added to the economic stress. As a child, Baluch and his family were forced to flee their village after heavy rains caused flooding, only to return weeks later to find their home gone. He recalls:

> When we got back, we found our house destroyed by the flood. . . There are hundreds of other places in Balochistan that get flooded almost every year and people . . . lose their lives, homes and livelihoods. Extreme heat and droughts are the other main factor for the climate crisis in Balochistan. People are being displaced, animals are dying, rare species are threatened with extinction. . . . This is the real climate emergency.[10]

Even though Pakistan contributes little to causing climate change, it is among the top ten nations most affected by it. Baluch says that most Pakistanis are not well informed about climate change or its impact on the country. He admits that he himself did not know a lot about the climate crisis until he heard Thunberg speak in 2019. Her words helped him understand the relationship between the extreme weather events that plagued Balochistan and climate change.

Inspired by Thunberg, Baluch founded an FFF chapter in Balochistan. As the chapter's leader, he organizes and leads rallies and weekly school strikes all over Pakistan. He hopes his campaign will pressure Pakistani lawmakers to focus on mitigating the effects of climate change in Pakistan. And, in an effort to get climate justice, he wants the Pakistani government, and those foreign nations and industries that are responsible for much of the environmental degradation, to build dams and reservoirs and replant trees in the region. So far, Baluch's campaign has had a positive impact. It has raised public awareness about climate change and encouraged the Pakistani

> "People are being displaced, animals are dying, rare species are threatened with extinction. . . . This is the real climate emergency."[10]
>
> —Yusuf Baluch, climate activist

> ## "Trash Girl"
>
> Nadia Sparkes has been picking up plastic litter on her way back and forth to school since she was a little girl. The Norwich, England, teen's actions caused her to be bullied by some of her peers, who dubbed her "Trash Girl." Their teasing has not deterred Sparkes. As she told reporters, "I'm not going to stop doing the right thing because of them, and if they are going to call me 'Trash Girl,' they can say it with respect. I'm doing something to protect the world they also live in."
>
> Indeed, Sparkes's actions have gained her the respect of many of her compatriots, inspired other members of her community to take positive actions, and won her a Points of Light award, an international award that recognizes people dedicated to helping society. As one of her Facebook followers wrote, "This young lady deserves recognition for the work she is doing to keep Britain tidy. She beat the bullies by being interviewed on TV. She kept going while being called names. She now wears the name 'Trash Girl' with pride and so she should."
>
> Quoted in James Hitchings-Hales and David Brand, "'Trash Girl' Nadia Sparkes Wins Award for Her Environmental Work," Global Citizen, April 11, 2019. www.globalcitizen.org.

government to plant millions of trees. Although a good start, Baluch thinks more needs to be done to end the crisis. Therefore, he keeps fighting. "This situation led me to speak against the injustice we are facing," he says. "We will not let our future or our children's future be destroyed!"[11]

Planting Trees in Uganda

Like Baluch, Ugandan native Leah Namugerwa (born 2004) lives in a developing region disproportionately affected by climate change, and she, too, was inspired by Thunberg. She remembers:

> It was the year 2018 when I first heard about Greta Thunberg from Sweden. I did not first understand what she was doing, given the fact that the word strike in Uganda is inseparable with violence. I asked my dad what school

strike for climate meant and he told me that Greta was not attending class every Friday to protest against her government inaction. I asked if what she was doing was possible in Uganda and his answer was yes. . . . I did not take his word seriously until I watched the news . . . which reported hunger in northern Uganda due to prolonged drought and landslides in Eastern Uganda that claimed many lives. The cause of the landslides was attributed to climate change.[12]

In response, Namugerwa began researching climate change and following Thunberg on Twitter. Supported and guided by her uncle, Tim Mugerwa, a prominent Ugandan environmentalist, she founded FFF Uganda in 2019. She started skipping school on Fridays and tweeting about the reason for her actions. Soon other young people joined her. However, protesting in Uganda can be risky. Members of Namugerwa's group have been chased and their placards destroyed by adults opposed to their actions. She also faces physical threats and the possibility of being arrested for demonstrating. But the young activist is unafraid. If she is arrested, she says that the publicity might help her cause by raising public awareness of the climate threat Uganda faces.

Namugerwa has taken other steps to reduce the effects of climate change. On her fifteenth birthday, instead of having a party, she planted two hundred trees. She urges other Ugandan youths to do the same on their birthdays. She is also campaigning to get plastic bags banned in Uganda. These bags litter waterways and city streets, clog drainage channels and irrigation systems, and kill fish that think they are food and try to eat them. The young activist plans to become an environmental scientist in the future so that she can gain a better understanding of the issues involved in protecting the earth. In the meantime, she continues campaigning for climate action and climate justice for Uganda, Africa, and the world.

Getting New Laws Enacted

Halfway around the globe, in Washington, DC, another teen climate activist, Jerome Foster II (born 2002), has been blogging, making speeches, and striking with FFF as part of his campaign for laws to combat climate change. Foster's parents have spent time protesting for civil rights. As a result, he has been surrounded by politics and activism all his life and has always been interested in environmental issues. In 2017, when Foster was just fifteen, he was chosen by National Geographic to go on an

Teen activist Jerome Foster speaks into a bullhorn at a climate change protest in New York City in 2021. As the youngest member of the White House Environmental Justice Advisory Council, Foster is helping shape US climate policy.

expedition to Iceland, where he witnessed the effects of climate change on receding glaciers. That experience made him determined to take action.

Upon returning home, Foster volunteered with various environmental organizations in an effort to learn as much as he could. And with the help of one of his high school teachers, he started the Climate Reporter, a digital magazine that serves as a platform for young climate activists to share their news and experiences. Foster's role as founder and editor in chief of the magazine put him in touch with other climate activists, including Thunberg. In fact, before Thunberg began her first strike outside of Sweden's parliament, she emailed Foster and other young climate activists, asking them to hold similar strikes. Foster remembers thinking that his participation would not have much impact, but in an act of solidarity, he started his own solo protests on Fridays outside of the White House. A year later, on September 13, 2019, Thunberg joined him in Washington, DC. Her presence brought thousands of climate strikers to the nation's capital and helped publicize Foster's work.

And work he did. During his junior year, while attending school, running the magazine, and holding weekly strikes, Foster became a congressional intern for Representative John Lewis. That experience taught him a great deal about government and politics. While working for Lewis (who died in 2020), Foster lobbied lawmakers for passage of the Climate Change Education Act, which would make environmental education a required subject in all American schools. As of January 2022 the bill had not yet been passed, but Foster was hopeful that it would be enacted in the future. In order to help make this happen, he launched and serves as director of OneMillionOfUS, an organization dedicated to registering and

> "It's still a daunting task, the task of stopping the climate crisis is still no easier. But I'm a lot more optimistic now. Yeah, I'm hopeful."[13]
>
> —Jerome Foster II, climate activist

encouraging young people to vote and speak out on issues such as climate change.

Since becoming an activist, Foster has consulted with government officials and been a featured speaker at climate change events worldwide. He also developed a virtual reality company that allows users to experience the effects of climate change virtually. In 2021 President Joe Biden appointed him to serve as the youngest member of the White House Environmental Justice Advisory Council, where Foster is helping shape US climate policy. Despite his busy schedule, Foster continues his activism. He explains, "It's still a daunting task, the task of stopping the climate crisis is still no easier. But I'm a lot more optimistic now. Yeah, I'm hopeful."[13]

CHAPTER TWO

Ending Gun Violence

On February 14, 2018, a troubled nineteen-year-old named Nikolas Cruz entered Marjory Stoneman Douglas High School in Parkland, Florida, and went on a deadly rampage. Armed with an AR-15 military-grade assault rifle, Cruz killed a total of seventeen students and staff members and wounded seventeen others.

School shootings had happened before, and they were becoming more and more common. After each tragedy, elected officials offered their condolences but did little else to address gun violence. Parkland survivors Sarah Chadwick, Jaclyn Corin, Emma González, David Hogg, Cameron Kasky, and Alex Wind, among others, were upset and angry that they could not count on lawmakers to protect them. So they decided to take matters into their own hands. They would use their voices to demand stronger gun control laws, including but not limited to a ban on military-grade rifles and the enactment of a law prohibiting people with a mental illness from buying guns. Kasky dubbed their mission #NeverAgain, and a movement was born.

Although the teens were not experienced activists, they were adept at using social media, which they used to get their message out. They also gave speeches, organized rallies, and talked to journalists and lawmakers about the massacre and the need for stricter gun control laws. In a short time they had become public figures, and word of their mission spread rapidly. Consequently, when they announced that they were holding a national school walkout on the one-month anniversary of the mass shooting, thousands of students all over the United States walked out of class and stood in silent protest for seventeen minutes (one minute for each victim) in solidarity with the Parkland students.

Keeping the momentum going, the Florida teens planned a national protest, which they called the March for Our Lives. It took place in Washington, DC, one week after the national school walkout. About eight hundred thousand people took part in the city's demonstration. Individuals in eight hundred cities around the world held similar protests in support of the movement. In all, 1 million to 2 million people participated, making the March for Our Lives one of the largest youth-led protests in history.

The impact of the young activists and the movement they created did not sit well with individuals and groups opposed to gun control. These people and organizations tried to discredit the youths. For instance, some conspiracy theorists accused the students of being paid actors. In addition, the teens were mocked and threatened on social media. Yet they stayed strong. Having faced death, they refused to be silenced. As Parkland survivor Leonor Muñoz asserted, "Our trauma isn't going away, but neither are we. We will fight every day because we have to, because change is the only thing that makes any of this bearable."[14]

After the March for Our Lives, the Parkland students continued their battle. Inspired by the civil rights freedom riders of the 1960s, during the summer of 2018, they went on what they called the Road to Change Tour. The teens traveled to fifty cities, where they met with other gun violence survivors and registered thousands of young voters before the upcoming elections. "We can have all the walkouts we want, but if we don't walk to that ballot box and make our voices heard, these politicians aren't going to listen," Hogg explained. "We need to vote people out of office that are perpetuating issues affecting young people, like gun violence."[15] Their efforts helped defeat forty-six National Rifle Association–backed candidates. It also raised public consciousness about gun violence. As a result, some stores stopped selling AR-15 rifles. Moreover, twenty-five states passed a total of fifty new gun control laws.

March for Our Lives has since grown from a one-day protest into a youth-led national movement, whose members work to make their schools and local communities safer. The Parkland teens are now young adults. Some have taken a break from organizing, while others continue fighting for change. In addition to

> "We need to vote people out of office that are perpetuating issues affecting young people, like gun violence."[15]
>
> —David Hogg, gun violence–prevention activist and Parkland school shooting survivor

The 2018 Parkland shooting inspired a group of teen survivors to organize March for Our Lives, a national protest against gun violence. Here, young protesters join the hundreds of thousands of people who marched in Washington, DC.

gun control, they battle for racial and social justice and try to address other issues that impact their lives. Plus, they have encouraged a new generation of young people to raise their voices and stand up for what they believe.

Gun Violence Seems Normal

The mass shooting that jump-started the #Never Again and the March for Our Lives movements was not without precedent. According to a report published in the *Washington Post*, since 1966, when a sniper killed seventeen victims at the University of Texas, more than thirteen hundred Americans have died in mass shootings. However, mass shootings, which are defined as a shooting in which at least four people are killed, account for only a small fraction of gun deaths and injuries. Gun-related injuries, homicides, and suicides receive less media coverage than mass shootings but affect thousands of Americans every year. Everytown for Gun Safety, a gun violence–prevention organization, reports that guns kill one hundred Americans and injure more than two hundred every day.

People of color, the poor, women, and other marginalized groups are especially vulnerable. According to the Centers for Disease Control and Prevention (CDC), Black children and teens are more than ten times more likely to die from gun violence than their White peers, mainly because they tend to live in low-income communities with high levels of crime. In a 2019 report, the CDC found that although Black males ages fifteen to thirty-four make up just 2 percent of the nation's population, they account for 37 percent of gun homicides. The report also found that Black females are at the highest risk of being killed by gun violence compared to females of any group. "Gun violence has for the longest time been a public health crisis in the Black community,"[16] explains epidemiologist Ed Clark of Florida A&M University's Institute of Public Health.

Although gun violence is not limited to the United States, the country ranks first among developed nations in gun-related

#Wear Orange

When Naomi Wadler spoke at the March for Our Lives protest in Washington, DC, she wore an orange scarf. A few months later, in October 2018, Wadler gave the keynote address at the Washington Area Women's Foundation annual leadership luncheon. Before the event, she shaved off most of her black curls and dyed her remaining hair orange.

Wearing orange in protest of gun violence began in 2015 when friends of Hadiya Pendleton wanted to commemorate what would have been Pendleton's eighteenth birthday. An innocent victim, Pendleton was shot and killed in a Chicago park in 2013. The shooter had mistaken her for someone else. Pendleton's friends chose to wear orange to honor her because it is the color hunters wear to avoid being shot by mistake. Had Pendleton lived, she would have celebrated her eighteenth birthday on the first Friday in June, which has now been named National Gun Violence Awareness Day.

Wearing orange to raise awareness about gun violence and to honor all gun violence victims and survivors has since become part of the gun violence–prevention movement. And Wadler's orange scarf is on display at the Smithsonian Institution's National Museum of American History.

---

deaths. Gun ownership is part of American culture. Per capita, Americans own more guns than any other nation. In 2020 alone, the Federal Bureau of Investigation reported that Americans purchased nearly 40 million guns. According to research published in the *American Journal for Medicine*, higher levels of gun ownership are linked to higher levels of gun-related deaths.

Gun control is a hot political issue in the United States. The Second Amendment of the Constitution grants Americans the right to bear arms. Many gun rights supporters believe that any gun control regulations are unconstitutional, and many politicians agree with them. As a result, young gun control activists face serious challenges from many sources. But that has not stopped them from battling to safeguard their own future and the future of those who come after them.

Losing a Brother

Personal experience with gun violence has motivated many young activists. Natalie Barden (born 2002) is a gun control activist whose life changed forever on December 14, 2012, when her younger brother, Daniel, was gunned down in a mass shooting at Sandy Hook Elementary School in Newtown, Connecticut. He was among twenty first-grade students and six staff members who were killed in the second deadliest school shooting in US history.

The tragedy took a massive toll on Barden, who was in fifth grade at the time, and on her family. In response to Daniel's death, Natalie's father became a gun control activist and wanted her to join his group, but at the time she refused. After her brother's murder, she spent years struggling with the trauma. "I never wanted to think about gun violence," she wrote in an essay for *Teen Vogue*. "I knew the importance of gun safety, and of course never wanted my tragedy to happen to anyone else, but as a kid, all I wanted was to be normal and not constantly reminded of my loss."[17]

The Parkland shooting changed Barden's mind. When she witnessed the courage of the Parkland survivors, she was inspired to speak out too. She writes, "I saw the teenagers down in Florida immediately speaking out for gun responsibility. It inspired me to do the same. I thought, if these kids are able to speak about this topic so soon after this tragedy, I can join them by adding my voice. . . I decided that I could no longer use these excuses. As much as I may want to be 'normal,' I'm not."[18]

Barden joined the Junior Newtown Action Alliance, a local gun violence–prevention club for youth, and gradually became more and more involved. She attended meetings and conferences, called lawmakers, gave interviews and speeches, organized voter registration drives, and wrote magazine articles. She attended the March for Our Lives. And when the Road to Change Tour stopped in Newtown, she met the leaders of the #NeverAgain movement personally.

As the sister of a mass shooting victim, Barden is often thrown into the spotlight. Now a college student, she still finds talking about her loss very difficult but feels it is worth the pain if she can keep others from going through what her family has endured. As she explains, "Unfortunately, I know what losing a loved one to gun violence feels like, and I think more should be done to prevent the lives of others from being shattered in that way."[19]

Never Too Young

Naomi Wadler (born 2006) is another gun control activist whose life has been touched by gun violence. As an infant, she was adopted from an Ethiopian orphanage and taken to live in Alexandria, Virginia. Her mother is White, and her father is Black. The family often watches the news together. Wadler has noticed racial bias in news reporting. It seemed to her that White victims of gun violence received more media attention and sympathy than Black victims. This disturbed her.

When the Parkland shooting occurred and she learned that a friend of her family was one of the victims, the eleven-year-old wanted to do something to honor that friend. And she wanted to recognize gun violence victims of color whose deaths were largely ignored. So she and her classmate, Carter Anderson, organized a walkout at their elementary school. Unlike other national school walkouts, which lasted seventeen minutes, Wadler added an extra minute to this walkout. That minute, she explained, was for Courtlin Arrington, a Black teenager who had recently been killed in an Alabama high school shooting and whose death had not received widespread attention.

Wadler's action caught the attention of news and social media outlets,

> "Unfortunately, I know what losing a loved one to gun violence feels like, and I think more should be done to prevent the lives of others from being shattered in that way."[19]
>
> —Natalie Barden, gun violence–prevention activist

The work of teen activist Naomi Wadler (second from right) has received worldwide attention. She is pictured here with school shooting survivors Emma Gonzalez (third from right) and Tyra Hemans (fourth from right) at a Washington, DC, rally against gun violence.

and two days before the March for Our Lives she was asked to speak at the event. She spent a full day writing a speech and worried about how it would be accepted. In the speech, she talked about Arrington and other young Black female victims of gun violence whose stories did not receive wide media coverage. "I represent the African-American women who are victims of gun violence, who are simply statistics instead of vibrant, beautiful girls that fill a potential," she told the crowd. "For far too long these names, these black girls and women have been just numbers. I'm here to say 'never again' for those girls, too."[20]

Wadler was the second-youngest speaker at the event. She was so small that she had to stand on a stepstool to be seen from behind the podium. People and organizations opposed to gun control tried to downplay her speech, saying she was too young to understand what she was talking about. But they were

Keeping It Local

While the #Never Again and March for Our Lives movements focus on changing state and national gun control policies, many young gun violence–prevention activists are battling to make their local communities safer. A group of Essex High School students in Essex Junction, Vermont, are tackling local gun safety issues head-on.

Vermont is a state where hunting is a popular pastime. According to Vermont senator Bernie Sanders, approximately half of all local households own guns. Unintentional shootings are common, especially when children get their hands on unsecured firearms and accidentally discharge the weapons. Indeed, according to the National Shooting Sport Foundation, secure firearm storage is essential to preventing unintentional as well as intentional shootings. Up to 80 percent of school shooters use unsecured guns that they find in their homes or the homes of family members, according to the US Secret Service's National Threat Assessment Center.

Therefore, as part of their mission, a group of Essex, Vermont, teens are demanding that local school boards enact policies that require schools to educate parents on safe firearm storage. They believe that storing guns unloaded in a locked cabinet with ammunition stored in a separate place will save lives.

---

unsuccessful. Her words went viral, shining a light on the connection between gun violence and racial inequality.

Wadler has become one of the most celebrated gun control activists in the world. She has made it her mission to speak out for all victims of gun violence and to battle for gun law reform. In the process, she has received many awards for her work. Now a high school student, she balances her school work with her activism, giving speeches and interviews and hosting *DiversiTea with Naomi Wadler*, a web series in which she talks with celebrities about issues facing young people today. She dreams of becoming a doctor, an actress, or the executive editor of the *New York Times* someday. Anything is possible; Wadler has proved that she will not be underestimated.

Sharing Information and Raising Awareness

Other gun control activists, such as Alé Ortiz (born 2004), are less well known than Wadler but are also working hard to make real change. In the Los Angeles neighborhood where Ortiz lives, the sound of gunfire is an everyday occurrence. Ortiz wants to end the violence. She explains, "The first time I heard gunshots, I thought they were fireworks—something that was supposed to be beautiful. But in my neighborhood . . . it was a year-round Fourth of July of gunfire. The shots seemed to be constant. It was never clear where they were coming from, who was shooting them, and if they would one day take the lives of my friends or family members."[21]

Ortiz is Latina and a member of the LGBTQ community. Studies show that these two groups experience disproportionate levels of gun violence. The vulnerability of these two groups puts Ortiz and others like her at risk.

Although Ortiz worried about her own safety and the safety of her friends and family, she still considered the violence around her as just part of everyday life. A 2016 mass shooting at Pulse,

In 2016, forty-nine people were killed in a shooting at Pulse (pictured days after the shooting, with security fencing covered in tributes), a gay nightclub in Orlando, Florida. The tragedy inspired activist Alé Ortiz to speak out against gun violence.

a gay nightclub in Orlando, Florida, changed her mind. She says, "When I heard about how 49 people were shot and killed at Pulse in Orlando, it felt like I had a target on my back. . . . I was scared to live in a country where so much hatred was directed at my community."[22]

Ortiz wanted to do something to help end gun violence but had no idea what to do or how to do it. Then in 2020 she joined the Students Demand Action Summer Leadership Academy, a program sponsored by Everytown for Gun Safety. The program helps students develop the skills they need to become gun violence–prevention activists. As part of the program, participants are required to develop a plan of action to reduce gun violence in their local communities. Ortiz came up with a plan for a podcast directed at educating listeners about gun violence prevention. She enlisted the help of her friends, Jamilex Soto and Julie Matamoros, and together they named the podcast *3 Homegirls No Gun*. Like Ortiz, Soto and Matamoros grew up surrounded by gun violence and wanted to help change things. The three hosts talk about the issues that surround gun violence and their own experiences with gun violence. They also interview other young people about their experiences, as well as experts on the subject. As Matamoros explains, "We've had some touching experiences with our guests because they always bring in something personal or how gun violence has impacted them."[23]

Although their audience is not large, the girls believe that it will grow. In the meantime, they plan to continue their advocacy in hopes of inspiring other teens to step up and speak out against gun violence.

CHAPTER THREE

Battling for Racial Justice

On May 25, 2020, George Floyd, an unarmed Black man, was killed by Derek Chauvin, a White Minneapolis police officer. The killing occurred when Chauvin tried to arrest Floyd for allegedly passing a counterfeit twenty-dollar bill. Police video suggests that Floyd did not act aggressively. Nevertheless, Chauvin felt it necessary to use force to restrain him. Floyd was handcuffed and forced to lie facedown on the ground. Chauvin then pressed his knee into Floyd's neck for more than nine minutes as three other officers looked on. Floyd repeatedly called out, "I can't breathe,"[24] and he begged for mercy, but the officers ignored his suffering, allowing him to suffocate. A seventeen-year-old witness recorded video of Floyd's last moments on her cell phone and posted it on social media, where it was played and replayed thousands of times. Chauvin was eventually convicted of murdering Floyd.

Floyd's murder affected many Black people who have witnessed or experienced police brutality and racial injustice in their daily lives. But it was not just African Americans who were appalled by the incident. People of all races and ethnicities took to the streets of Minneapolis to protest the killing and to support Black Lives Matter (BLM), a political and social movement

Minneapolis police officer Derek Chauvin (on right) is pictured at his trial for the murder of George Floyd. Floyd's murder inspired worldwide protest against racial injustice committed by the police.

championing racial equality and police reform. The protests spread all over the world and continued throughout the summer. A 2020 Civis Analytics poll estimated that 15 million to 26 million people, many of whom were youths, participated in the protests in the United States alone.

An Ongoing Problem

What happened to George Floyd is not an isolated incident. Racism and racial injustice have plagued the United States and many other nations for centuries. Throughout US history, White Americans have enjoyed privileges and rights related to, but not limited to, education, voting, employment, and criminal justice that members of other racial and ethnic groups have been denied. The Civil Rights Act of 1964 was created to end these inequities.

However, even in the twenty-first century, people of color often face unequal treatment, especially by the police and the criminal justice system. This is especially a problem for Black Americans, who are more likely to receive harsher treatment by law enforcement officers than Whites are. A four-year study of police killings, published in 2020 by the Harvard T.H. Chan School of Public Health, found that Black Americans are more than three times as likely to be killed during a police encounter as White people are. And in some cities, the disparity is even greater. Black people in Chicago, for example, are more than 650 percent more likely to be killed by police than their White counterparts are.

Occurrences of police violence, racially driven violence, and racial injustice toward Black people led to the formation of the BLM movement. It was started in 2013 in response to the shooting and killing of Trayvon Martin, an unarmed Black teenager, by a White man who claimed that he shot the young man in self-defense. Many teen activists are members of local BLM chapters. These young activists have made it their mission to put an end to systemic racism, including organizing protests against police brutality toward African Americans.

A Born Activist

Thandiwe Abdullah (born 2004) is one of these young activists. Abdullah, who is Black and Muslim, lives in Los Angeles. Even before she was born, members of her family were standing up for racial equality. Her grandmother was active in the Black Power movement of the 1960s, and her mother is a cofounder of Black Lives Matter Los Angeles. Abdullah was just two years old when her mother took her to her first protest rally and ten years old when she started accompanying her mother to BLM meetings.

Questioning and battling racial injustice is part of Abdullah's heritage. By the time she was in middle school, she too was speaking out against racial injustice. Giving voice to societal wrongs, however, did not endear her to her teachers or peers. It marked her as different. She recalls:

> When I began doing movement work it was hard. I fell quickly into the angry Black girl mold created for me by society. I called out teachers at school and never let anyone slide when using the "N word." . . . I was lit up, and for some reason it seemed like all everyone around me wanted to do was shut me up. . . . It wasn't cool to be a revolutionary . . . but I constantly reminded myself of the why. I did the work for justice, and that kept me going.[25]

One of her earliest battles began in 2016. In order to provide students with a safe learning environment, police officers were stationed in Los Angeles secondary schools, where they frequently conducted random searches of students. As part of these searches, the officers pulled students out of class; rummaged through their lockers, backpacks, and purses; and confiscated personal items like lipsticks, perfumes, and pens, for no clear reason. Abdullah noticed that the Black, Hispanic, and Muslim students were searched more frequently and more thoroughly than other students. She also noticed that when the police found low-level contraband, like a joint or a pocketknife, they turned the White students over to school officials for disciplinary action. In contrast, they arrested the Black students.

Rather than making everyone feel safe, these searches traumatized many students of color, including Abdullah. She vowed to take action. With the help of the Los Angeles BLM chapter and Students Deserve, a local student advocacy organization, Abdullah battled for more than three years to get police searches banned on Los Angeles school campuses. She rallied her peers, attended school board meetings, wrote letters, contacted lawmakers, and met with school district leaders. In June 2020

Young Civil Rights Heroes

Teens and young adults have battled against racial inequality and injustice for many years. Many served on the front lines in the civil rights movement of the 1960s, despite the dangerous pushback they faced.

In 1961, for example, two courageous nineteen-year-old students, Charlayne Hunter-Gault and Hamilton Holmes, became the first Black students to attend the University of Georgia. White students made it clear that the two were unwelcome. When Hunter-Gault arrived on campus, she was greeted by a mob screaming racial slurs. That night, about two thousand rioters amassed outside her dorm room, which was isolated from those of White students. The rioters threw rocks and soda bottles through her window and threatened her life. Holmes, who was able to live off campus with a Black family, was also threatened. The university suspended them both for their involvement in the riot.

Despite the danger that attending the university posed, the two young people continued their fight. They obtained a court order forcing the school to readmit them five days later. Their battle paved the way for other Black students to attend the university.

---

she helped organize a protest outside the Los Angeles Unified School District's administrative offices. Thousands of students and BLM supporters participated. Many of the student protesters were members of the BLM Youth Vanguard, an organization that Abdullah and her younger sister, Amara, founded to help Black youths organize against racism in schools. As a result, officers have been removed from some campuses, and funding for those remaining has been cut significantly. She is also responsible for helping develop Black Lives Matter at Schools, an antiracism education program that has been adopted by Los Angeles public schools and by a major labor organization, the National Education Association.

Abdullah also participated in Los Angeles' BLM protests following Floyd's murder. She was part of a group that shut down a freeway and were attacked by counterprotesters. She is also active in other movements, which she says intersect with her battle against racism. For instance, she participated in and spoke at the Los Angeles March for Our Lives, where she read the names of Black youths who were shot and killed by police officers around the nation. "Black Lives Matter is not an isolated cause," she insists. "The liberation of black people is about the liberation of all oppressed people: other people of color, poor folks, immigrants, queer folks and trans folks. I think that message gets lost oftentimes."[26]

> "Black Lives Matter is not an isolated cause. The liberation of black people is about the liberation of all oppressed people: other people of color, poor folks, immigrants, queer folks and trans folks. I think that message gets lost oftentimes."[26]
>
> —Thandiwe Abdullah, teen activist

Black Lives Matter was formed in response to police violence, racially driven violence, and racial injustice. Here, participants at a 2020 rally in Los Angeles protest the deaths of people of color at the hands of the police.

Abdullah vows to continue her fight for justice. Her ultimate goal is to transform society, thereby creating a more just world. As she explains, "I want to see a world where folks don't have to worry about not affording basic human needs like food, shelter, education, medical care. I want a world where police aren't militarized. . . . I want everyone to care about other people. I want people to think that their own success and justice is tied to everyone around them."[27] Following in her mother and grandmother's footsteps, the lifelong activist intends to keep speaking out until her vision becomes a reality.

Keeping Everyone Safe

Whereas Abdullah has been fighting to end racial injustice for most of her life, Stefan Perez (born 2004) had never taken part in a demonstration before George Floyd's killing. When Perez decided to participate in Detroit's BLM protests in June 2020, he did not expect that he would become a leader in the movement. But as a mixed-race youth who had witnessed racial injustice for most of his life, he decided it was time to make his voice heard.

Perez grew up in a neighborhood where crime, gang violence, and police brutality are daily occurrences. He experienced many tragedies in his short life, losing friends and family members to crime, violence, and a racially biased criminal justice system. He was homeless for a time. Due to all he witnessed and experienced, he did not think he would live to be sixteen, much less become a leader in the BLM movement. He turned to music—writing and performing rap songs about racial injustice—to cope with the challenges he faced. As he recalls, "My first few raps that I actually wrote around sixth grade were directed towards civil rights and activism. I used to write about how it's unfair that we have to live like this. I talked about social injustices and systematic oppression we must endure on a day-to-day basis because of the color of our skin."[28]

Standing Up by Sitting Down

Most school days in the United States begin with students standing and reciting the Pledge of Allegiance. In an effort to draw attention to racial injustice, some young activists have refused to participate in this daily ritual. Although a 1943 Supreme Court ruling protects students from being punished for refusing to say the Pledge of Allegiance, it is not uncommon for students to be reprimanded for their actions.

Chanice McClover-Lee, a young BLM activist, is one of these students. She describes her experience in her book, *Young Revolutionary: A Teen's Guide to Activism*:

> As a Black teenager, I didn't feel the words "liberty and justice for all" applied to me due to all the injustices I witnessed. . . . Throughout the school year, no one ever asked me why I didn't say the Pledge, but they did give me looks. Looks that screamed, "What is wrong with you?" and "Why aren't you saying the Pledge?!" . . . I must admit it did bother me at first. Sometimes I thought to myself, "Am I making the right choice?" Overall, I did not let the looks get to me and I continued to stand firm in my beliefs.

Chanice McClover-Lee, *Young Revolutionary: A Teen's Guide to Activism*. Chanice Lee in partnership with YBF Publishing, 2018, p. 91.

After Floyd's murder, he felt like he had to do more. So, on the fourth day of Detroit's BLM protests, he took a city bus to the protest site and joined a small group of demonstrators who were beginning to march. Someone handed Perez a megaphone. As the group moved forward, Perez used the megaphone to urge other marchers and bystanders to join them. Soon about two thousand protesters were marching behind Perez and looking to him for leadership.

To avoid trouble, the city had instituted an 8:00 p.m. curfew. However, the curfew had actually caused trouble on the previous night. When protesters refused to keep the curfew, a violent clash erupted between the police and the demonstrators. Perez did not want this to happen again. He wanted to keep his followers safe. He thought the best way to do this was to send people home in a timely fashion. So, shortly before 8:00, when the group was met by a line of armed police officers, Perez inserted himself between the two groups before any trouble could erupt. He fell to his knees, raised a fist in the air, and using the megaphone urged the demonstrators to abide by the curfew and go home. The protesters trusted Perez. So they listened to him and went home, thereby avoiding what could have turned into a bloody confrontation between protesters and police. "I tried to keep everybody together," he told the *Detroit Free Press*. "I tried to keep everybody as a collective group, and we marched. I'm surprised people listened to me. I'm glad they did because they're not hurt right now, 'cause they could be."[29]

Once the crowd cleared, Perez caught a city bus and went home, too. But before he did, a man who was at the protest and knew the mayor handed Perez a phone. Detroit mayor Mike Duggan, who had been monitoring the protest on video, was on the other end. Duggan was almost in tears when he thanked Perez for his leadership and praised him for his actions. In response, Perez told the mayor, "I just wanted to make sure everybody got home safe. I'm not going to lie to you now. We are going to hold more marches and protests, but I am going to make sure we are safe. That we end up safe. That I get people home. . . . It is not about how long you can stay in the fight. It is about how many times you can win. And today was a win because we didn't lose anybody."[30]

Perez has kept his promise. He led multiple peaceful protests throughout that summer. In addition, he has become an advocate for homeless people, giving them food and water whenever he can. When asked about the future, he said, "In five years, I hope to be alive. I hope to see the people

> "It is not about how long you can stay in the fight. It is about how many times you can win."[30]
>
> —Stefan Perez, teen activist

Stefan Perez is pictured at a BLM protest that he helped lead in Detroit in 2020. At this, and subsequent, demonstrations, Perez worked to prevent violence between protesters and police.

that I've marched with and fought with and continuously done this stuff with alive also. I just hope that we can continuously build a future for ourselves."[31]

Teens 4 Equality

Around the time Perez was leading marchers in Detroit and Abdullah was protesting in Los Angeles, an estimated ten thousand BLM supporters, most of whom were teens and young adults, marched through Nashville, Tennessee, in what was named the Teens 4 Equality March. That demonstration was organized in less than a week by six teenagers: Nya Collins, Jade Fuller, Kennedy Green, Emma Rose Smith, Mikayla Smith, and Zee Thomas, who were ages fourteen to sixteen at the time. The young women had no previous experience as activists. Yet the five-hour demonstration that they organized went off without a hitch.

Their story began when Thomas, shaken by Floyd's killing, decided to speak out. Inspired by the protests taking place throughout the country, she wondered why similar demonstrations were not being held in Nashville. Although she had no experience as an activist, she made up her mind that she would organize a local protest march. She doubted that she could do this alone; as a matter of fact, she had no idea how to organize a protest march. So she went on Twitter asking for assistance. The other teens responded right away, offering to help.

Most of the six teens had never met. But their shared disgust with the racial injustice that plagued the United States bonded them. "As teens, we are tired of waking up and seeing another innocent person being slain in broad daylight," Thomas explains. "As teens, we are desensitized to death because we see videos of black people being killed in broad daylight circulating on social media platforms. As teens, we feel like we cannot make a difference in this world, but we must."[32]

Planning and meeting via FaceTime, group chats, and Instagram, the youths named their coalition Teens 4 Equality. They developed a list of goals and then they reached out to established organizations for guidance about how to proceed. The Nashville BLM chapter offered the youths advice about how to organize the event and posted its support on social media, urging its followers to turn out for the protest march. But it was the six young women working together who would be ultimately responsible for the rally's success or failure.

On June 5, when the six teens arrived at the protest site, it was the first time they had all met face-to-face. But after spending the past few days as almost constant virtual companions, they felt like old friends. They did not know what to expect and worried that no one would show up for the protest. However, their worries were needless. By the time the event was scheduled to start, the

> "As teens, we feel like we cannot make a difference in this world, but we must."[32]
>
> —Zee Thomas, teen activist

area was filled with people. Although the six teens were nervous about their role as protest leaders, each gave a speech before they led the marchers to the state Capitol.

The protest was just the start of the teens' battle against racial injustice. Since then, they have organized and led other demonstrations in the Nashville area. And Teens 4 Equality has grown to about twenty-eight thousand followers. The teenage founders have pledged to continue working for change and are optimistic about the future. "A new revolution is on the way," they wrote on Instagram. "The world of racism, police brutality, and ignorance is ending, and a new world is blossoming. ALSO to everyone asking this is not the end. Stay tuned for more news, stuff is on the way."[33]

CHAPTER FOUR

Improving Children's Lives

When Leslie Arroyo (born 2002) was a freshman in high school in Adelanto, California, she read a memoir written by Malala Yousafzai. Yousafzai is a famous Pakistani activist whose fight for girls' rights to an education has grown into an international movement. Before reading Yousafzai's memoir, Arroyo had not known that in some parts of the world, females face restrictions related to education because of their gender. These girls' plight outraged Arroyo. She felt compelled to do something about it. "I . . . was shocked to realize that so many girls around the world did not have the opportunity to get the education they rightfully deserved. I then realized that I had to be a voice for these girls such as Malala is. I knew I may have not wealth or much of a platform, but I had to find a way to make an impact in these girls' lives and give them the education they rightfully deserved,"[34] she explains.

Like many other beginning activists, Arroyo did not know how to proceed. When she learned about Girl Up, a United Nations initiative dedicated to improving the lives of girls, she decided to start a chapter in her high school. Through Girl Up's online resources she learned how to organize and lead events.

Using her new skills, she became a national teen adviser for the organization. In this position, she trained other girls to become activists, and she raised money to fund Girl Up chapters throughout the world. Her goal is to break down the barriers that many girls face. "Just because 130 million girls are out of school at the moment it does not mean that it has to stay that way," she insists. "Instead I can set out and make a difference in this world."[35]

> "Just because 130 million girls are out of school at the moment it does not mean that it has to stay that way. Instead I can set out and make a difference in this world."[35]
>
> —Leslie Arroyo, girls' education activist

Harmful Customs

Customs that exploit children and deny them basic human rights are common in many parts of the world. Practices such as child labor and child marriage interfere with a young person's access to education. Other traditional beliefs about the role of women in society keep girls out of school or limit their educational opportunities.

Lack of education keeps young people from reaching their full potential and negatively impacts society. An education increases a person's employability and earning potential, which helps lift individuals, families, communities, and nations out of poverty. According to the World Bank, limited educational opportunities for girls cost countries $15 trillion to $30 trillion in lost productivity and earning. Not surprisingly, nations with low literacy rates are also among the poorest.

Despite the value of an education, in many parts of the world, instead of attending classes, children do the work of adults. The International Labor Organization, a United Nations agency, reports that in 2021, 152 million children ages five through seventeen were child laborers. These boys and girls work in manufacturing, mining, farming, fishing, and domestic service, among other jobs. Many face hazardous conditions that put their health and safety at risk. In the Democratic Republic of the Congo, for example, an estimated thirty-five thousand children are involved in cobalt mining. Their work exposes them to toxic fumes that cause lung disease. Compounding the problem, in some parts of the world, children are sold into bonded labor by their parents as a repayment for a debt. This practice, which is similar to slavery, is illegal in most nations. However, laws banning bonded child labor are frequently ignored in parts of Africa and Asia.

Child marriages also curtail a child's education. These marriages are rooted in age-old traditions, cultural beliefs, and gender inequality. They are typically between young girls and older males. Child marriages negatively impact a girl's physical and mental well-being. Child brides are frequently abused by their

Child labor is common in many countries, and often has negative impacts on children's health. Here, young girls work to recycle trash in a slum in the Philippines.

husbands. If they become pregnant, according to the CDC, they face a high risk of developing health complications or dying during childbirth due to their age.

Many young activists are working to ensure that all children have access to an education. They are battling to end child marriage and child labor. These young people are challenging cultural norms, which puts them in danger. Often, they are threatened and attacked by people who hold fast to age-old traditions. For example, in 2012 Yousafzai was the victim of a vicious, near fatal assassination attempt in retaliation for her activism.

Changing a Village

Payal Jangid (born 2002) is one of these fearless young activists. She lives in Hinsla, an impoverished village in India, where child labor and child marriages are deeply ingrained in the local culture. When she was eleven years old, her parents arranged for her to be married. This plan upset Jangid. She believed that marrying at such a young age was wrong. She wanted to continue her education so that she could become a teacher someday. Getting married would end her schooling and destroy her dream. She shared her predicament with a children's rights activist who visited her school. With the activist's support, Jangid convinced her parents to call off her wedding. Then she took on the mission of defending the rights of other children. Her goal was to keep all the children in her village in school by putting an end to child marriage and child labor, both of which are illegal (but still practiced) in some parts of India.

She went door-to-door informing children about their legal rights. She also spoke with parents and village leaders about how allowing children to stay in school benefits families and communities. She organized rallies to raise awareness of the importance of education. At first, she faced fierce opposition. Many parents barred her from talking to their children. Others accused her of

Payal Jangid campaigns to defend the rights of children in India. She is pictured here (at right) with then US president Barack Obama, First Lady Michelle Obama, children's rights activists Kailash and Sumedha Satyarthi, and two children the activists work with.

filling their children's heads with fanciful ideas. Some insulted and threatened her. But she kept on.

Her determination paid off. Within one year of the start of her campaign, there were no more child marriages in her village, and more children were attending school. Moreover, with her urging, her village established a child parliament with Jangid as its head. Child parliaments are found in many nations. They are made up of young people who discuss matters that affect the rights and welfare of children and present their views to village leaders. As the head of the children's parliament, Jangid is helping create a safe environment for her peers.

In recognition of her role in bringing positive changes to her community, Jangid was awarded the Bill and Melinda Gates Foundation Changemaker Award in 2019. This award is given annually to young people dedicated to creating a better world.

Since then, Jangid has not stopped battling for children's rights around the globe. As she asserts, "I want every kid in the world without education to be helped and given a chance to progress in society."[36]

> "I want every kid in the world without education to be helped and given a chance to progress in society."[36]
>
> —Payal Jangid, children's rights activist

Turning Filmmaking into Activism

Jangid's activism began when her ability to continue her education was threatened. Even when children are not forced to work or marry, in some parts of the world, not all children attend school. Girls, in particular, are frequently denied access to education. The United Nations Children's Fund (UNICEF) reports that an estimated 132 million girls worldwide do not attend school. Girls are kept out of school for a number of reasons, including sociocultural beliefs that restrict a female's freedom. In Afghanistan, for example, since the Taliban, an ultraconservative Islamic group, gained control of the country in August 2021, most secondary schools for girls have been closed. Meena Sadat, an Afghani girl whose education has been cut short as a consequence, notes that her country is struggling with a question that should have been settled long ago: "This is the 21st century. The world is focused on issues such as climate change, technology and science. Yet in Afghanistan, we are still talking about whether women deserve an education."[37]

Girls who attend school often become targets of attacks, both in class and walking to and from school. These threats, along with poverty, keep many girls out of school. Attending school often requires students to pay for books, school supplies, and transportation. According to the World Bank, if families have trouble affording these costs, they are more likely to send boys, who are seen as future breadwinners, to school, rather than girls.

The statistics support the conclusion that girls face significant barriers to education in many parts of the world. In Pakistan, for instance, an estimated 22 million children are out of school. The majority are girls. Similarly, according to Africa Educational Trust, an organization devoted to educating African children, less than 2 percent of girls in Somalia attend secondary school, and by grade five twice as many boys as girls attend school in Uganda and Kenya.

Many teen activists are raising their voices to end this inequity. Zuriel Oduwole (born 2002) is one of these voices. Oduwole is a young filmmaker who lives in Los Angeles but has roots in Africa. Her father is Nigerian, and her mother is Mauritanian. She uses her skills in filmmaking in her mission. In fact, her rise to prominence began in 2012, when she made a

Children's Rights

In 1989 the United Nations adopted the Convention on the Rights of the Child. It is an international treaty that sets the rights that children and adolescents up to age eighteen are entitled to so that they can reach their full potential. According to UNICEF, "The Convention establishes in international law that States Parties [governments] must ensure that all children—without discrimination in any form—benefit from special protection measures and assistance; have access to services such as education and health care; can develop their personalities, abilities and talents to the fullest potential; grow up in an environment of happiness, love and understanding; and are informed about and participate in, achieving their rights in an accessible and active manner."

In an effort to achieve these goals, the convention set up minimum standards for governments to follow. The treaty has been ratified by 165 nations, which means these nations agree to follow these standards. Even so, some of these governments flout the standards, making it imperative that children's rights activists raise awareness and advocate for the young.

UNICEF, "Frequently Asked Questions on the Convention on the Rights of the Child." www.unicef.org.

documentary film about Ghana for a competition sponsored by the History Channel. It was her first attempt at filmmaking. She traveled to Ghana to make the film. While there she met many poor African girls who did not attend school but, rather, tried to earn money to help their families—which in many cases allowed their brothers to get an education. As she recalls, "I saw a lot of children, especially girls, out on the streets selling things and I see that a lot whenever I visit other African countries like Nigeria, Ethiopia and Tanzania. . . . In many African countries, boys tend to be first in line when resources are scarce. And that's not cool."[38]

This inequity troubled her. When, as part of the film, she interviewed Ghana's former president Jerry Rawlings, she asked for his help in solving the problem. In the following months, while filming a second documentary, she met with the presidents of Malawi, Mauritius, and Tanzania, and once again she advocated for girls' education. Still, Oduwole wanted to do more. So in 2013 she launched Dream Up, Speak Up, Stand Up, a program designed to encourage girls to stay in school, urge world leaders to expand girls' education, and raise public awareness of the value of educating girls. As part of the program, Oduwole met with and gained the support of more than thirty world leaders. She also enlisted the support of her younger sisters, Azaliah and Arielle. The three girls traveled to thirteen nations, where they spoke to girls in orphanages and schools about the importance of education.

Oduwole also continued making award-winning films about life in Africa. In 2015 she got the idea of teaching basic filmmaking to poor, unemployed African youth, so that they could gain marketable skills that would help them get good-paying jobs. She believes that education should be practical and therefore not limited to traditional academic classes. As she explains:

> I first started it [filmmaking classes] when I was 13 years old in Namibia, and that was just my pilot project. I taught

some girls and youth—25 and under. I taught them some basic filmmaking skills because I believe that education isn't just learning in the classroom, it's also about learning skills that you can use to benefit yourself. And so because I'm a filmmaker, I can teach other youth in Africa to tell their stories. And if they can, make a living off of filmmaking.[39]

Oduwole's filmmaking classes turned out to be so popular that she now offers them on three continents. Although she entered Harvard University when she was just sixteen years old, she has not slowed down. She is still making films and meeting with world leaders. Oduwole insists that, when it comes to advocating for girls' education, she is unstoppable.

Malala Yousafzai

Malala Yousafzai (born 1997) is probably the most renowned girls' education activist in the world. The Pakistani girl began her activism in 2008 when the Taliban, a militant ultraconservative group that opposes educating females, occupied the region in which she lived. When the Taliban banned girls in the region from attending school, she started an anonymous blog describing her life under the repressive regime.

Once the Pakistani army had taken back control of the region, Yousafzai became the subject of a documentary film. Her blogging identity was revealed, and she began appearing on international television to promote her campaign. This was dangerous. The Taliban still had many followers in the region, and she received numerous death threats. In 2012 a Taliban member shot her in the head in a near fatal attempt on her life. She spent four months in the hospital after the shooting.

Upon recovering, she continued her work. In 2014 she was awarded the Nobel Peace Prize. Since then, she has written a memoir and founded the Malala Fund, an organization that supports girls' education throughout the world. And she serves as an inspiration for other young activists.

Standing Up for Educational Equity

Unfortunately, even when girls have access to education, in many places there are large gender gaps between the education they receive and that of their male peers. In many countries it is common for boys and girls to attend separate schools. Generally, schools for boys have better facilities than those for girls. The course of study often differs, too. As a consequence of negative gender stereotypes, girls are often discouraged from studying STEM subjects, which people in some parts of the world consider to be too difficult for girls. This misconception causes many girls to avoid STEM classes even when they have access to them. According to Girl Up, only one in three students enrolled in STEM classes are female. This discrepancy impacts the well-being of girls later in life, since having STEM skills can significantly increase a person's employability and earning potential.

Silicon Valley resident Samaira Mehta (born 2008) is one of a number of young activists tackling this issue. Her father, who is an engineer, taught her to code when she was just six years old. Coding is a process that is used to create computer software, websites, and apps. Mehta thought coding was fun and wanted to share it with her friends. But they were not interested. To pique their interest, she invented a board game called CoderBunnyz that teaches players coding concepts in a simple and entertaining way. It combines all of Mehta's favorite things—coding, bunnies, and board games.

She tested the game on her friends. They loved playing it and quickly learned basic coding concepts. Metha's mother suggested that she use the game to teach other children to code, so Mehta went to local libraries and schools offering her services. However, because of her age, she was not taken seriously. In fact, she was told to come back in a few years. Nevertheless, she persisted, and the Santa Clara Public Library took her up on her offer. Her workshop was a huge success, and it was not long before Mehta was giving workshops all over Silicon Valley.

Around the world, millions of girls are denied access to education. Teen activists are working to help change that. This 2021 picture shows a secret school in Afghanistan, where most secondary schools for girls have been closed by the Taliban.

When she started leading these workshops, Mehta was unaware of the STEM education gender gap. But as she led more and more sessions, she noticed that the vast majority of participants were male. In order to bridge this gap, in addition to her co-ed workshops, she began Girls U Code. It is an initiative offering coding workshops just for girls that has proved to be very popular. "I want it [STEM education] to be equal," she explains. "Girls should not be scared to try something new."[40]

In the next few years, Mehta created two more board games, which introduce players to programming and artificial intelligence concepts. As her success grew, so did her goals. She wanted to get her games into the hands of as many children, and especially girls, as possible. Therefore, with her parents' help, she started a business named CoderBunnyz that made her games available for purchase by consumers. Mehta, who serves as the business's chief executive officer, donates some of the profits to charity. In addition, she and her younger brother, Aadit, created a campaign known as Yes, One Billion Kids Can Code (YOBKCC). It aims to teach 1 billion children how to code by 2030. YOBKCC partners with private donors—corporations like Walmart and tech companies like Microsoft—to get Mehta's games to impoverished communities all over the world. In addition, the campaign sponsors workshops, competitions, and clubs for young people. So far, over 1 million children worldwide have learned coding and other STEM concepts using Mehta's games.

Although still very young, Mehta has already accomplished more than many adults. "I believe age is just a number." she says. "If you have ideas, no matter how old you are, you have the power to change the world."[41] The actions of brave and inspiring young activists throughout the world who have made a commitment to causes that matter to them are proof that she is right.

> "I believe age is just a number. If you have ideas, no matter how old you are, you have the power to change the world."[41]
>
> —Samaira Mehta, inventor, STEM education activist, and entrepreneur

SOURCE NOTES

Introduction: Powerful Voices

1. Chanice McClover-Lee, *Young Revolutionary: A Teen's Guide to Activism*. Chanice Lee in partnership with YBF Publishing, 2018, p. 15.
2. Jamie Margolin, *Youth to Power: Your Voice and How to Use It*. New York: Hachette, 2020, p. xvii.
3. Margolin, *Youth to Power*, p. xviii.

Chapter One: Protecting the Earth

4. "IPCC Report: 'Code Red' for Human Driven Global Heating, Warns UN Chief," United Nations, August 9, 2021. https://news.un.org.
5. Quoted in Tribal Gatherings, "Tribes." www.tribalgathering.com.
6. Quoted in Goodreads, "Greta Thunberg," 2022. www.goodreads.com.
7. Quoted in Karla Montalván, "Greta Thunberg Opens Up About Her Personal Transformation and New Outlook on Life," *People*, September 28, 2021. https://es-us.vida-estilo.yahoo.com.
8. Quoted in David Crouch, "The Swedish 15-Year-Old Who's Cutting Class to Fight the Climate Crisis," *The Guardian* (Manchester, UK), September 1, 2018. www.theguardian.com.
9. Quoted in Amy Goodman, "Greta Thunberg Says It's Time to Wake the Adults Up," Truthout, September 11, 2019. https://truthout.org.
10. Yusuf Baluch, "Living with the Crisis in Balochistan," Naya Daur, April 8, 2021. https://nayadaur.tv.
11. Quoted in Atlas Sarrafoğlu, "Yusuf Baluch: The Flood in Balochistan Destroyed Our Home," Yeşil Gazete, September 1, 2021. https://yesilgazete.org.
12. Quoted in Earthday.org, "A Day in the Life of Ugandan Student Striker Leah Namugerwa," June 6, 2019. www.earthday.org.
13. Quoted in Oliver Milman, "'I'm Hopeful': Jerome Foster, the 18-Year-Old Helping to Craft US Climate Policy," *The Guardian* (Manchester, UK), April 13, 2021. www.theguardian.com.

Chapter Two: Ending Gun Violence

14. Quoted in Truth School, "Standing in Solidarity with March for Our Lives," March 17, 2018. https://truthschool.org.
15. Quoted in WHQ World, "Top 46 David Hogg Quotes," October 20, 2020. https://whqworld.com.
16. Quoted in Nada Hassanein, "Young Black Men and Teens Are Killed by Guns 20 Times More than Their White Counterparts, CDC Data Shows," *USA Today*, February 23, 2021. www.usatoday.com.
17. Natalie Barden, "Natalie Barden Reflects on the Sandy Hook Shooting, the March for Our Lives, and Why She Still Fights for Gun-Violence Prevention," *Teen Vogue*, August 15, 2018. www.teenvogue.com.
18. Barden, "Natalie Barden Reflects on the Sandy Hook Shooting, the March for Our Lives, and Why She Still Fights for Gun-Violence Prevention."
19. Barden, "Natalie Barden Reflects on the Sandy Hook Shooting, the March for Our Lives, and Why She Still Fights for Gun-Violence Prevention."
20. Quoted in i-D, "How Naomi Wadler Is Going to Change the World," August 30, 2018. https://i-d.vice.com/en_uk/article/9km8x5/how-naomi-wadler-is-going-to-change-the-world.
21. Alé Ortiz, "Gun Violence Is a Queer Issue," Students Demand Action, July 1, 2021. https://studentsdemandaction.org.
22. Ortiz, "Gun Violence Is a Queer Issue."
23. Quoted in Everytown for Gun Safety, "Inspiring Others to Take Action Through the *3 Homegirls No Gun* Podcast," July 30, 2021. www.everytown.org.

Chapter Three: Battling for Racial Justice

24. Quoted in Maanvi Singh, "George Floyd Told Officers 'I Can't Breathe' More than 20 Times, Transcripts Show," *The Guardian* (Manchester, UK), July 9, 2020. www.theguardian.
25. Thandiwe Abdullah, "I March for Black Girls & the Black Women Who Marched Before Me," Refinery29, 2019. www.refinery29.com.
26. Quoted in Rachel Janfaza, "Across the Country, Young Activists Take Different Approaches in the Name of Justice for George Floyd," CNN, June 3, 2020. www.cnn.com.
27. Quoted in Madison Feller, "These Teen Black Lives Matter Activists Are Writing the Future," *Elle*, July 20, 2020. www.elle.com.
28. Quoted in Isla Davis, "Meet the 16-Year Old Who Got Thousands Home Safely After Protesting," Very Good Light, June 17, 2020. https://verygoodlight.com.

29. Quoted in Branden Hunter, "16-Year-Old Emerges as a Leader at Detroit's Monday Protest: 'I Felt I Made a Mark,'" *Detroit (MI) Free Press*, June 2, 2020. www.freep.com.
30. Quoted in Fox 2, "16-Year-Old Stefan Perez Helps Lead Peaceful Night of Protest in Downtown Detroit," June 2, 2020. www.fox2detroit.com.
31. Quoted in Davis, "Meet the 16-Year Old Who Got Thousands Home Safely After Protesting."
32. Quoted in Elyse Wanshel, "Teen Girls Organized a 10,000-Person Black Lives Matter Protest in Nashville," HuffPost, June 10, 2020. www.huffpost.com.
33. Quoted in De Elizabeth, "As Teens We Are Tired of Waking Up, and Seeing Another Innocent Person Being Slain in Broad Daylight," *Teen Vogue*, June 7, 2020. www.teenvogue.com.

Chapter Four: Improving Children's Lives

34. Quoted in Darling Team, "The Youth Rise Up: Part 1 with Girl Up," *Darling* (blog), May 17, 2018. https://blog.darlingmagazine.org.
35. Quoted in Darling Team, "The Youth Rise Up."
36. Quoted in Press Trust of India, "Rajasthan Teen Gets 'Changemaker' Award from Gates Foundation," NDTV, September 26, 2019. www.ndtv.com.
37. Quoted in Fatema Hosseini and Kim Hjelmgaard, "Hidden Books, Secret Meetings, Precious Hope: In Afghanistan, Girls Risk It All for an Education," *USA Today*, November 22, 2021. www.msn.com.
38. Quoted in Theirworld, "At Just 15, Zuriel Has Talked About Girls' Education to 24 Presidents and Prime Ministers," September 22, 2017. https://theirworld.org.
39. Quoted in Jane Nyingi, "Teen Activist Zuriel Oduwole: 'Education Is More than Learning in Class,'" DW, November 10, 2018. www.dw.com.
40. Quoted in Katy Steinmetz, "Eight Young Leaders on How They Want to Shape the Decade Ahead," *Time*, January 16, 2019. https://time.com.
41. Quoted in Alexis Nichols, "11-Year-Old Coder Samaira Mehta on Reverse Ageism, Gender Gap," Parentology, October 29, 2019. https://parentology.com.

ORGANIZATIONS AND WEBSITES

Amnesty International
www.amnestyusa.org
Amnesty International is a human rights organization. Teens can volunteer with the organization as student activist coordinators. Volunteers learn about government policies and gain organizational and activism skills. They are involved in organizing rallies, lobbying, fundraising, and letter-writing campaigns.

Black Lives Matter
https://blacklivesmatter.com
Black Lives Matter is an organization that fights for justice and equality for Black people, with local chapters throughout the world. It provides many resources to educate and help activists organize.

Do Something
www.dosomething.org
Do Something is a large youth-led organization working for social change. Through its digital platform, members are able to join a variety of campaigns related to causes that they care about. Members can earn scholarships through community service.

Everytown for Gun Safety
www.everytown.org
Everytown for Gun Safety is the largest gun violence–prevention organization in the United States. It sponsors Students Demand Action, a movement of high school and college student activists working to end gun violence. Students Demand Action members educate their peers, register voters, and organize in their local communities.

Fridays for Future

https://fridaysforfuture.org

Fridays for Future is a youth-led international climate strike organization. It offers information about climate change, future strikes, how to strike, resources and materials, and opportunities to connect with other climate activists.

Girl Up

https://girlup.org

Girl Up is an international organization sponsored by the United Nations, with chapters all over the world. It is dedicated to advancing girls' and women's rights, opportunities, and leadership skills. It educates members on important issues and trains them to become activists and leaders.

Youth Activism Project

https://youthactivismproject.org

The Youth Activism Project trains teens in community organizing. It instructs teens on planning and organizing protests and rallies, helps them get involved in lobbying, provides action guides, and connects teens with mentors and other activists.

FOR FURTHER RESEARCH

Books

Anna Collins, *Student Rights in a New Age of Activism*. New York: Lucent, 2020.

Stuart Kallen, *Teen Guide to Student Activism*. San Diego, CA: ReferencePoint, 2019.

Jamie Margolin, *Youth to Power*. New York: Hachette, 2020.

Margaret Rooke, *You Can Change the World! Everyday Teen Heroes Making a Difference Everywhere*. Philadelphia: Jessica Kingsley, 2019.

Internet Sources

Amnesty International USA, "How to Get Involved in Activism for the First Time," *Teen Vogue*, January 2, 2019. www.teenvogue.com.

Anti-Defamation League, "Ten Ways Youth Can Engage in Activism," 2022. www.adl.org.

Jessica Bennett, "These Teen Girls Are Fighting for a More Just Future," *New York Times*, June 26, 2020. www.nytimes.com.

Ellen Cranley, "These 10 Young Activists Are Trying to Move the Needle on Climate Change, Gun Control, and Other Global Issues," Insider, 2019. www.insider.com.

Tina Donvito, "14 Incredible Kids Who Changed the World in the Last Decade," *Reader's Digest*, July 29, 2021. www.rd.com.

INDEX

Note: Boldface page numbers indicate illustrations.

Abdullah, Thandiwe, 33–37
activism
  among teens, history of, 5
  aspects of, 6–7
Africa Educational Trust, 49
American Journal for Medicine, 24
Amnesty International, 58
Anderson, Carter, 26
Arroyo, Leslie, 43–44

Baluch, Yusuf, 13–15
Barden, Daniel, 25
Barden, Natalie, 25–26
Biden, Joe, 19
Bill and Melinda Gates Foundation, 47
Black Lives Matter at Schools, 35
Black Lives Matter (BLM) movement, 31–32, 36, 58
bonded child labor, 45

Centers for Disease Control and Prevention (CDC), 23, 46
Chadwick, Sarah, 20
Changemaker Award (Bill and Melinda Gates Foundation), 47
Chauvin, Derek, 31, **32**
child laborers, 44–45, **45**
  numbers of, 44
child marriages, 45–46
Children's March (1963), 5
Civil Rights Act (1964), 32–33
Clark, Ed, 23
Climate Change Education Act (proposed), 18
Collins, Nya, 40
Convention on the Rights of the Child (UN, 1989), 49
Corin, Jaclyn, 20
Cruz, Nikolas, 20

Detroit Free Press (newspaper), 39
DiversiTea with Naomi Wadler (web series), 28
Do Something, 58
Dream Up, Speak Up, Stand Up program, 50

education
  costs of limiting girls' access to, 44
  number of girls worldwide not attending school, 48
  STEM, encouraging girls to enroll in, 52–54
Everytown for Gun Safety, 23, 58

Federal Bureau of Investigation, 24
Floyd, George, 31, 37

Foster, Jerome, II, **17**, 17–19
Fridays for Future (FFF), 12, **13**, 59
Fuller, Jade, 40

girls
   encouraging enrollment in STEM classes by, 52–54
   numbers not attending school worldwide, 48
Girls U Code, 53
Girl Up, 43–44, 52, 59
González, Emma, 20, **27**
Green, Kennedy, 40
gun ownership, in US, 24

Hemans, Tyra, **27**
Hogg, David, 20, 21–22

Intergovernmental Panel on Climate Change (United Nations), 8
International Labor Organization, 44

Jangid, Payal, 46–48, **47**

Kailash, Satyarthi, **47**
Kailash, Sumedha, **47**
Kasky, Cameron, 20
Kennedy, John F., 5

Lewis, John, 18

Malala Fund, 51
Mandamin, Josephine, 4
March for Our Lives (2018), 21, **22**, 28
Margolin, Jamie, 7
Marjory Stoneman Douglas High School shooting (Parkland, FL, 2018), 20, 25
Martin, Trayvon, 33

mass shootings, number of Americans killed in, 23
Matamoros, Julie, 30
McClover-Lee, Chanice, 5, 38
Mehta, Aadit, 53–54
Mehta, Samaira, 52–54
Mugerwa, Tim, 16
Muñoz, Leonor, 21

Namugerwa, Leah, 15–16
National Education Association, 35
National Shooting Sport Foundation, 28
National Threat Assessment Center (US Secret Service), 28
#Never Again movement, 20, 23, 28
No One Is Too Small to Make a Difference (Thunberg), 9

Obama, Barack, **47**
Obama, Michelle, **47**
Oduwole, Arielle, 50
Oduwole, Azaliah, 50
Oduwole, Zuriel, 49–51
opinion polls. *See* surveys
Ortiz, Alé, 29–30

Peltier, Autumn, 4–5, **6**, 7, 8
Perez, Stefan, 37–40, **40**
police killings, racial disparity in, 33
polls. *See* surveys
Pulse nightclub (Orlando), **29**
   2016 mass shooting at, 29–30

racial disparities
   in gun homicides, 23
   in police killings, 33
Rawlings, Jerry, 50
Road to Change Tour (2018), 21–22, 25

Sadat, Meena, 48
Sanders, Bernie, 28
Sandy Hook Elementary School shooting (Newtown, CT, 2012), 25
Smith, Emma Rose, 40
Smith, Mikayla, 40
Soto, Jamilex, 30
Sparkes, Nadia, 15
Students Demand Action Summer Leadership Academy, 30
Students Deserve, 34
surveys
 on climate change, 8
 on numbers participating in BLM marches, 32

Teens 4 Equality movement, 40–42
Teen Vogue (magazine), 25
T.H. Chan School of Public Health (Harvard University), 33
Thomas, Zee, 40, 41
3 Homegirls No Gun (podcast), 30
Thunberg, Greta, 9, 10–12, **13**, 14, 15–16, 18
Trudeau, Justin, 4

United Nations Children's Fund (UNICEF), 48, 49

Wadler, Naomi, 24, 26–28, **27**
Washington Post (newspaper), 23
Wildcat, Jazmine, 5–6
Wind, Alex, 20
World Bank, 44, 48

Yes, One Billion Kids Can Code (YOBKCC), 53–54
Young Revolutionary (McClover-Lee), 38
Yousafzai, Malala, 43, 46, 51
Youth Activism Project, 59

PICTURE CREDITS

Cover: Vanessa Nunes/iStockphoto

6: macri roland/Shutterstock.com
10: polybutmono/Shutterstock.com
13: Liv Oeian/Shutterstock.com
17: Associated Press
22: Nicol Glass Photography/Shutterstock.com
27: Reuters/Alamy Stock Photo
29: Anthony Constantine/Shutterstock.com
32: ZUMA Press/Alamy Stock Photo
36: Hayk_Shalunts/Shutterstock.com
40: ZUMA Press/Alamy Stock Photo
45: John Christian Fjellestad/Shutterstock.com
47: Reuters/Alamy Stock Photo
53: Associated Press